The Truth About Your Food

# Be Smart About Factory Foods

By Rachael Morlock



Cavendish Square

Published in 2023 by Cavendish Square Publishing, LLC
2544 Clinton Street, Buffalo, NY 14224



Website: cavendishsq.com



Cataloging-in-Publication Data

Names: Morlock, Rachael.
Title: Be Smart About Factory Foods / Rachael Morlock
Description: New York : Cavendish Square, 2023. | Series: The Truth About Your Food| Includes glossary and index.
Identifiers: ISBN 9781502665751 (pbk.) | ISBN 9781502665768 (library bound) | ISBN 9781502665775 (ebook)
Subjects: LCSH: Food –Juvenile literature. | Food industry and trade –Juvenile literature.
Classification: LCC TX355 M67 2023 | DDC 641.3–dc23

Editor: Rachael Morlock
Copyeditor: Shannon Harts
Designer: Deanna Paternostro

The photographs in this book are used by permission and through the courtesy of: Cover (main) Andrew Makedonski/Shutterstock.com; cover (DNA graphic), back cover, pp. 3, 4, 7, 10, 14-15, 20, 25, 27, 35, 40, 42-43, 44-45, 46-47, 48 Omelchenko/Shutterstock.com; p. 5 monticello/Shutterstock.com; p. 6 Giancarlo Polacchini/Shutterstock.com; p. 9 Bitenkav2/Shutterstock.com; p. 11 urbans/Shutterstock.com; p. 12 Jonathan Oscar/Shutterstock.com; p. 14 maradaisy/Shutterstock.com; p. 17 Africa Studio/Shutterstock.com; p. 19 Niloo/Shutterstock.com; p. 21 Ivaschenko Roman/Shutterstock.com; p. 22 eldar nurkovic/Shutterstock.com; p. 24 Rosamar/Shutterstock.com; p. 26 Microgen/Shutterstock.com; p. 29 Marie-Claude Lemay/Shutterstock.com; p. 31 Nickolas warner/Shutterstock.com; p. 32 Goncharov_Artem/Shutterstock.com; p. 34 Vladislav Noseek/Shutterstock.com; p. 36 Brent Hofacker/Shutterstock.com; p. 37 Ahmet Misirligul/Shutterstock.com; p. 39 Monkey Business Images/Shutterstock.com; p. 41 The Image Party/Shutterstock.com



CPSIA compliance information: Batch #CWCSQ23: For further information, contact Cavendish Square Publishing LLC at 1-877-980-4450.

Printed in the United States of America

# Contents

# Introduction

Food is a complicated subject. The number of opinions about how and what people should eat is very surprising, especially for such a basic part of human life. Although there have been many scientific advances in how we understand food and nutrition, there's a lot we still don't know. It's hard to pinpoint exactly what it is about fruits and vegetables that make them so beneficial to health. Scientists and doctors are still discovering how foods interact with our body systems. What is clear is that choosing some foods over others can lead to better long-term health.

The foods that show the greatest benefits for our health are called whole foods. For the most part, whole foods come to you straight from the ground or from the animal. They are not processed, or changed very much, before being eaten. They may be cooked, frozen, or chopped up, but their substance is basically the same. Fruits, vegetables, and eggs are examples of whole foods.

When foods are changed substantially before being eaten, they are called processed foods. Most processed foods are made in factories, so they are sometimes called factory foods. Factory food has been chemically changed in order to create a product for sale. Some factory foods undergo a lot of changes before being sealed up and shipped to restaurants and stores. These highly processed foods use many ingredients to boost their flavor, appearance, and appeal. Often, they have preservatives that allow them to last for a long time. Although factory foods are

Healthy meals generally contain whole, unprocessed foods like fruits and vegetables.

often tasty, they are less healthy than whole, unprocessed foods. Many are high in fat, sodium, and sugar. If eaten too often, they can sometimes lead to serious and lasting illnesses.

Factory foods aren't all bad. People buy them because they are fast, convenient, and often cheap. Having the occasional factory food is generally not cause for concern, but loading your meals and snacks with heavily processed foods can be harmful. In the United States, 60 percent of the **calories** in the average person's diet come from highly processed foods. This is a big problem that has already caused a lot of health issues for Americans. Learning how to spot factory foods is a good step toward building a healthier future.

Thanks to hamburgers, beef is one of the most common foods on the American menu. The average American eats 55 pounds (25 kilograms) of beef each year.

# Chapter One

## Factory Foods

Over 600,000 different processed foods are made and marketed in the United States. This overwhelming variety includes a range of quick snacks, frozen meals, and sweet desserts. Some are lightly processed and contain only a few ingredients. Some are heavily processed with long lists of additives, or substances like coloring added during processing, and high amounts of fat, sodium, and sugar. Factory foods include processed foods from stores and fast foods from restaurants. Many factory foods have become staples in our cupboards and on our tables. Some of the most common are hamburgers, french fries, tacos, soda, cereal, fried chicken, and pizza. This chapter looks at common factory foods, the ingredients that go into them, and the way that eating them affects you.

### Fast-Food Burgers

Hamburgers can be made from meat that is raised without the use of antibiotics and hormones. It can be served on a whole grain bun with toppings such as romaine lettuce or spinach and slices of tomato and onion. It takes several minutes to cook a hamburger and serve it on a plate with freshly sliced toppings.

However, fast-food hamburgers are a different story. They are usually made from high-fat meat that is ground up. About 80 percent of beef in the United States is killed and processed for food by four giant companies. In their meatpacking factories, the bits of meat from hundreds of carcasses are ground together, shaped into patties, and frozen. The patties are then shipped all across the country to stores and restaurants.

Once they reach a fast food restaurant, most patties are fried in grease on a griddle and kept warm until a kitchen worker places the patties on buns made from bleached white flour. A squirt of sweet ketchup and a sprinkle of mechanically diced onion often contain additives like food dyes. The few shreds of iceberg lettuce that are sometimes added have almost no nutritional value. The fast-food version of a hamburger may be easy to buy, but it's less nutritious than a homemade meal.

## Fries

French fries from fast-food restaurants aren't cut from fresh potatoes like the homemade version. Commercially made french fries are lightly boiled, frozen, and then packaged to be trucked hundreds of miles to various restaurants. In some factories, french fries are shaped out of cooked mashed potatoes. The french fries of one popular fast food chain contain 19 ingredients, including additives that are used to control the flavor, color, and texture of the fries.

Restaurants cook frozen fries in vats of hot fat—animal or vegetable oils such as pork lard, beef fat, peanut oil, corn oil, or canola oil. Different oils can affect the taste of fries. For people with food restrictions, it's important to know what kind

Factory-made fries can contain many additives that affect their flavor.

## Fast Food

Many people don't make their own pizza or chicken nuggets. They go to fast-food restaurants to get these foods. Take-out foods may seem similar to home cooking, but look carefully! Restaurants often use twice as much salt—or more—as anyone does at home. Corn syrup is a sweetener made from the sugars in corn. It is added to pizza sauce and to batter-fried chicken. Only a few restaurants have recipes with little or no salt and sweeteners added.

Companies that make fast food and processed food spend a lot of money on advertising. It's important to think critically about what we see in advertisements. Often, these ads do not focus on the food itself, but on how cool or fun you'll seem if you drink a certain soda or eat a certain type of fast food. Ask yourself: What is being sold in this ad—real food or an attitude?

It's very unusual to see an advertisement for lettuce, strawberries, or carrots. These natural foods do not need to be part of an ad campaign to get people to buy them.

of oil is used. Vegetarians will want to choose fries cooked in vegetable oils. If it's not included on the menu, you can ask a server about the type of frying oil they use.

## Sweet Drinks

Sweet drinks are popular factory foods that play a big role in the American diet. However, the sodas, juices, flavored milks, iced teas, and energy and sports drinks made in factories are packed with sugar. For most people, drinks are the biggest source of sugar in their diet.

The average can of soda has around 10 teaspoons (39 grams) of sugar. Drinking just one can each day adds a lot of

A surprising amount of sugar is found in soda. Satisfying your sweet tooth with 100 percent fruit juice will help you avoid added sugars.

empty calories to a person's diet. These calories are called empty because they do not include any nutritional value. The American Heart Association suggests that children and teenagers should have less than 6 teaspoons (25 g) of sugar a day, so one can of soda can quickly put you over the limit. Regularly having sweet drinks can lead to health problems such as heart disease, tooth decay, diabetes, and obesity. Occasional sugary drinks won't harm you, but they should be enjoyed in moderation. A glass of water or milk with meals is a healthier option for regular consumption. When you drink milk, you are ingesting calories as well as **vitamins**, minerals, and protein.

## Cereals

A bowl of cereal is a simple, fast breakfast. However, it's a good idea to read the ingredients listed on the box. Many packaged cereals have two or three times as much sugar and salt as people would add to the oatmeal, porridge, or granola they

Bright breakfast cereals that change the color of your milk are probably loaded with artificial dyes and flavors, not to mention sugar.

make at home. Artificial food coloring and flavoring are added to some cereals to make them interesting to children. Packaged cereal is also often made from bleached white flour, not whole wheat flour, which means the grain it is made from has had nutrients and minerals removed. Corn flour, sweeteners made from corn, and salt are usually added. There are also chemical preservatives, which aren't needed for bags of dry rolled or steel-cut oatmeal, cornmeal, or cracked grain porridge. Some packaged cereals are made from healthier whole wheat, but look carefully at the rest of the ingredients! Even whole-grain cereals can be packed with unhealthy sugars.

## Food for Thought

1. Food is important to most celebrations. Are the special foods you eat processed or whole?
2. Some schools have removed soda from their cafeterias to encourage healthier choices. How much say should schools have in what students eat and drink?
3. Some packaged foods use buzzwords to increase their appeal. Are you and your family more likely to choose foods labeled "whole grain" without checking the rest of the ingredients?

# Nutrition Facts

6 servings per container

**Serving size** **1 cup (230g)**

**Amount per serving**

## Calories 250

| | **% Daily Value*** |
|---|---|
| **Total Fat** 12g | **14%** |
| Saturated Fat 2g | **10%** |
| *Trans* Fat 0g | |
| **Cholesterol** 8mg | **3%** |
| **Sodium** 210mg | **9%** |
| **Total Carbohydrate** 34g | **12%** |
| Dietary Fiber 7g | **25%** |
| Total Sugars 5g | |
| Includes 4g Added Sugars | **8%** |
| **Protein** 11g | |
| Vitamin D 4mcg | 20% |
| Calcium 210mg | 16% |
| Iron 4mg | 22% |
| Potassium 380mg | 8% |

Added sugars are measured in grams on a nutrition facts label. You'll find this information listed below the amount of total sugars in one serving of a processed food.

# Chapter Two

## What's in Factory Foods?

You can make healthy choices while still eating factory foods. The important thing is to pay attention to how often you're eating them and what's in them. Learning how to read the nutrition facts label can help you choose factory foods with fewer fats, sugars, and additives, as well as lower amounts of sodium. Our bodies need a lot of nutrients to grow and be strong, but these substances should be eaten in small amounts.

### Added Sugars

Many whole foods have a natural supply of sugar. For example, lactose is a form of sugar found in milk, and fructose is a sugar that is a natural part of fruit. Some vegetables, grains, and nuts also contain natural sugars. These foods are not only sweet, but they're also high in **fiber**, vitamins, and minerals. Fiber helps the body digest sugar slowly.

Unlike natural sugars, added sugars are processed sweeteners that can be easily mixed with other foods. They do not bring any nutrients to food. Instead, they are used to improve flavor. There are more than 200 names for added sugars used in factory foods.

High-fructose corn syrup, also called corn sugar, is in many factory foods. Instead of filling you up, eating foods with high-fructose corn syrup can actually make you more hungry. In response, you might choose to eat more frequently, which can lead to weight gain. High-fructose corn syrup can also damage your liver over time.

Eating too much of any added sugar may cause serious health problems, such as diabetes and obesity. However, added sugars are found in 80 percent of processed foods. Even if you can't remember all the different names for added sugars, you can still find them on a nutrition facts label. These labels now record the amount of added sugar in one serving of factory food. This is an easy way to find out if the food you're eating has natural sugars, added sugars, or both.

## Names for Added Sugars

| Names with "Sugar" | Names with "Syrup" | Names with "-ose" |
|---|---|---|
| cane sugar | maple syrup | maltose |
| brown sugar | malt syrup | sucrose |
| raw sugar | corn syrup | dextrose |
| malt sugar | high-fructose corn syrup | fructose |
| | | glucose |
| | | lactose |

You can track down added sugars in a list of ingredients by looking for these common names.

## Fats

One problem with processed foods is fat. Many factory foods either have too much unhealthy fat or too little healthy fat to feed your whole body. Healthy fats—unsaturated fats like those

Trans fats are found in baked goods made with shortening or margarine. You can avoid trans fats by baking with butter instead.

found in avocados and fish oil—provide important fuel for your body and brain, especially while you're growing. Eating too many low-fat foods can keep you from getting the fats you need.

Saturated fats and trans fats, on the other hand, can have negative effects on your health. Trans fats come from oils that have been hydrogenated by adding hydrogen atoms to fat. They are found in many packaged foods, such as frozen pizzas, cookies, and buttery spreads. Trans fats have been linked to high blood sugar, high amounts of bad cholesterol, and low amounts of good cholesterol. Cardiovascular diseases related can also be traced to diets high in trans fats.

| **Unsaturated Fat** | **Saturated Fat** | **Trans Fat** |
|---|---|---|
| fish | fatty meat | margarine |
| avocado | butter | shortening |
| nuts | palm oil | |
| sunflower oil | coconut oil | |
| soybean oil | cream | |
| canola oil | cheese | |
| olive oil | ghee | |
| | lard | |

For a healthy diet, aim to eat foods with more unsaturated fat, less saturated fat, and no trans fat.

The World Health Organization is working to stop the industrial production of foods with trans fats around the world by 2023.

## Sodium

Sodium is a mineral that can be found naturally in some fruits, vegetables, and legumes. However, it is more commonly found in the compound sodium chloride, or salt. Most of the sodium in your diet comes from added salt.

Humans have been salting their food for thousands of years to preserve and flavor it. Today, salt is an important ingredient

Canned soup is traditionally very salty, but you can look for low-sodium options at the grocery store.

in factory foods that helps them last longer on the shelf and taste delicious.

Having a supply of iodized salt in your diet is good for your health. Iodized salt is sodium chloride that has been **fortified** with iodine, an essential element for

## Reading the Label

What's in your food? When you buy factory foods at a grocery store, you can find out by reading the nutrition facts label on the side or back of the package. The U.S. Food and Drug Administration (FDA) requires food manufacturers to label their products.

If you have food allergies, be sure to check the list of ingredients for anything that might cause an allergic reaction. Ingredients are listed in order of amount from most to least, including additives. In general, foods with shorter ingredient lists are less processed. Look for ingredients that you recognize as whole foods and avoid lists with many hard-to-pronounce names.

The serving size will tell you how much of the food should be eaten at a time. The information below the serving size breaks down the nutritional value of one serving. This is where you can pay attention to how much saturated fat, sodium, and sugar you're eating. The label also tells you the daily value of these nutrients by percent. This tells you how much of each nutrient you should be getting a day. Finally, important vitamins and minerals are listed at the bottom of the label.

thyroid health. The thyroid is a gland found in the neck that helps to control growth.

Your body needs salt, but you can get too much of a good thing! If many of the foods you eat each day are packaged, it can be easy to cross the line. Eating too much sodium can cause high blood pressure, heart problems, and damage to your kidneys. The World Health Organization recommends eating no more than a teaspoon, or 5 grams, of salt each day.

### Additives

Artificial ingredients added to processed foods are often called additives. Artificial coloring, like food dyes, are additives

Some factory-made jars of pickles and banana peppers use Yellow Dye 5 to preserve the vibrant color.

designed to make food look good. Preservatives are additives intended to increase the shelf life of processed food. Chemical flavorings are used to guarantee a certain taste. Texturing and thickening agents are meant to control the way food feels in your mouth.

The FDA investigates many of the chemicals and additives used in food. It has decided that these substances are safe to eat in small amounts, but that doesn't mean they are good for your body. The FDA has labeled some chemical additives as Generally Recognized as Safe (GRAS). This means that small amounts in food are thought to be safe, but the effects of eating

People who have food allergies have to read labels very carefully. The most common food allergies are to corn, soy, nuts, dairy, eggs, seafood, and gluten.

chemical additives regularly or over time are unknown. For example, types of yellow dyes and red dyes lend brilliant colors to food, especially those marketed to children, but they have been linked with cancer and allergies. Even though chemical additives are considered safe, they are best eaten sparingly.

## Allergens

Factory foods can be especially risky for people who have allergies. Most processed and restaurant food contains the common **allergens** corn, soybeans, wheat, and milk products. Factories often process many different foods, which can lead to contamination. Factories that process peanuts can accidentally contaminate other products when they use the same machinery.

People with food allergies have to be extra careful about what they eat. Some people have hives and stomachaches for weeks after unknowingly eating food with an allergen. People who are severely allergic to nuts or seafood can become seriously ill or die from very small amounts of these allergens.

## Food for Thought

1. Do you think it's important to read nutrition labels? Does knowing what's in your food affect your desire to eat it?
2. If additives are Generally Recognized as Safe (GRAS), then why do some people want to avoid them?
3. Do food producers have a responsibility to protect people with food allergies?

Even whole fruits and vegetables can carry dangerous bacteria. Be sure to wash fresh fruits and vegetables before eating them.

# Chapter Three

## Problems with Factory Food

Getting too much of your daily diet from factory foods can cause problems for your health, for animals, and for the planet. Foodborne diseases are illnesses that infect humans and animals through the foods they eat. The Centers for Disease Control and Prevention (CDC) estimates that one in every six Americans becomes sick every year from preventable foodborne illnesses.

Regularly eating foods high in fat, sodium, and sugar can make you more likely to experience obesity, type 2 diabetes, cardiovascular disease, and cancer. These diseases are especially high in Western countries, like the United States, where processed foods make up a large part of the average daily diet. Switching to whole foods has many benefits for your health and for the planet too.

### Making Food Safe

Governments try to make food safer by passing laws and regulations. Food can be contaminated with bacteria at any

Safety checks by food inspectors can help prevent outbreaks of foodborne diseases.

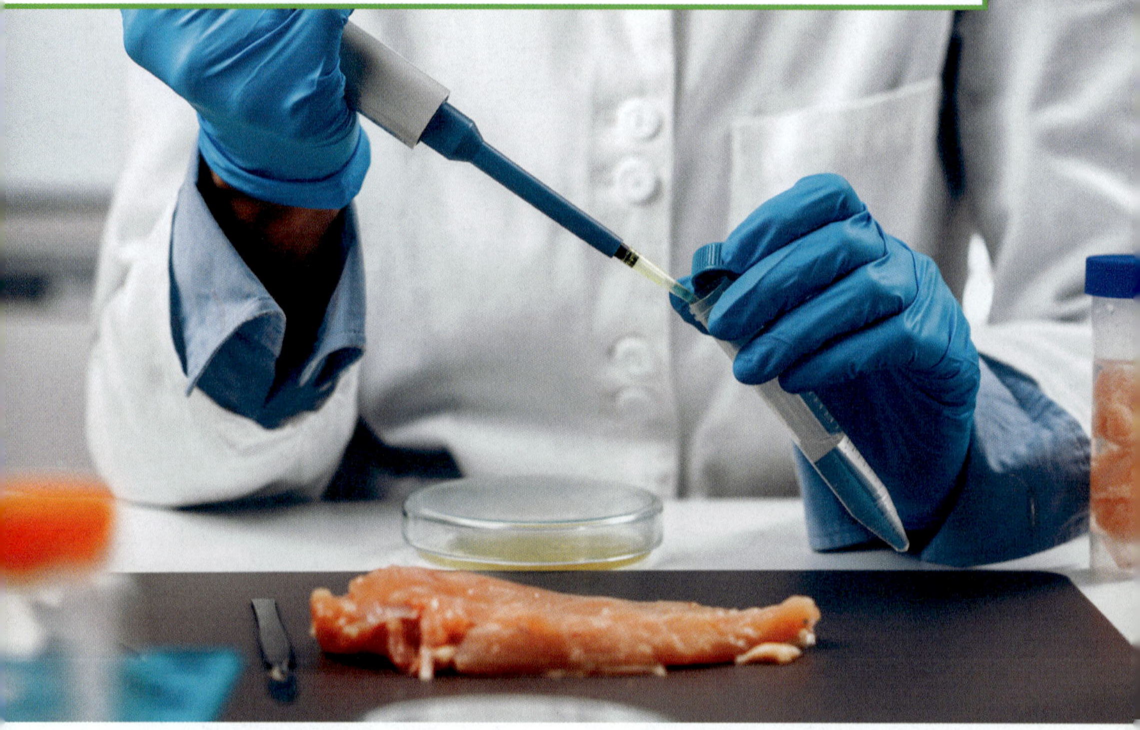

point during the production, processing, distribution, or preparation phases. Food safety rules are supposed to ensure that food is free from harmful substances and germs.

If food is not kept at the correct temperature, germs can begin to grow and cause foodborne illnesses. These germs can grow in hot food that's kept barely warm before being served or cold food that's kept at room temperature instead of in a refrigerator. It can be a challenge to keep each food item at the correct temperature until it is served.

Workers must have clean hands or clean gloves, and the kitchen must be kept clean. It's not enough to have laws about clean hands, clean kitchens, and the appropriate temperature to store and serve food. Restaurants and factories must be inspected regularly so experts can make sure food is handled properly.

## Foodborne Diseases

Foodborne diseases can cause mild symptoms that quickly go away, or they can cause serious health problems or death. These diseases are a concern in factories where large batches of food are prepared and then widely distributed. By the time

## Antibiotic-Resistant Bacteria

Antibiotics are powerful medicines for treating or preventing diseases in humans, animals, and plants. The feedlots of large factory farms are crowded with animals who can quickly spread diseases to each other. Dosing animals with antibiotics is one way to prevent and manage these diseases. However, the overuse of antibiotics has caused an increase in antibiotic-resistant bacteria. This is harmful bacteria that cannot be killed by antibiotics.

Bacteria in the food supply can make people very sick. The increase in antibiotic-resistant bacteria means that medicines are less likely to work to cure diseases. According to the U.S. Centers for Disease Control and Prevention (CDC), more than 35,000 people die each year from antibiotic-resistant **infections**.

Meat producers have a responsibility to control the spread of antibiotic-resistant bacteria. They can pledge to use antibiotics only when necessary, as determined by a veterinarian. As a buyer, you can look for meat labels that say no antibiotics were used in raising the food-producing animals. In addition to using fewer antibiotics, meat producers must also be very clean. Antibiotic-resistant bacteria usually enter the food supply through animal fecal matter. Meat processors must develop and follow careful guidelines for producing meat that is free from dangerous **pathogens**.

bacteria is discovered, the food could have already been eaten by many people in many different places. In response to an outbreak of people getting sick, food products that might be contaminated are **recalled** and people are warned not to eat them.

Some of the most common illness-causing bacteria in food are ***Salmonella***, *Campylobacter*, and *Shigella*. Food poisoning from *Salmonella* or other germs can cause long-term complications, such as reactive arthritis, also known as Reiter's syndrome. This illness causes inflamed joints, eyes, and urethra. The deep, aching pain is often severe and requires hospitalization. Symptoms of severe arthritis can be permanent.

***Escherichia coli***, more commonly called *E. coli*, can cause food poisoning and a few days of discomfort, with nausea, vomiting, and diarrhea in healthy people. The more severe form known as *E. coli* 0157:H7 may cause bloody diarrhea and life-threatening kidney failure. Other foodborne illnesses are norovirus and botulism.

Some foodborne illnesses are spread on contaminated machines and surfaces in factories, where food is cut and packaged. *Listeria* is usually found in soil and water and can spread on fresh fruits and vegetables or meat. People who eat meat with *Listeria* get very ill if the meat hasn't been cooked at a high enough temperature to kill the bacteria. Milk is **pasteurized** to kill bacteria and prevent illness.

Food preparers must have clean hands when working in a factory, restaurant, or at home. Otherwise, they can contaminate food with hepatitis A virus, *Shigella*, or *Staphylococcus aureus* bacteria. Careful hand washing can prevent these illnesses.

You should wash your hands for 20 seconds before, during, and after preparing food. Make one last trip to the sink to scrub before eating!

## Health and Diet

Eating mostly fast food and processed food creates an unhealthy diet that can make you sick. An upset stomach is a sign that the food you ate is difficult to digest, but processed food can cause more than just discomfort. Long-term constipation and diarrhea lead to more serious health problems. Diseases like type 2 diabetes, heart disease, and certain cancers are higher among people who eat a highly processed diet. These are **chronic** conditions that cause a lot of pain and can be deadly.

Cancer and other illnesses are usually the result of many different factors interacting with each other, such as your genetics, your lifestyle, and the environment you live in. Food is only one part of the picture. However, it's clear that there are fewer cases of cancer in people who eat more fruits and vegetables every day rather than highly processed foods. It's hard to make healthy choices because it can take a long time to see results. Still, choosing to eat whole foods often is something we have control over and that can have a huge benefit to our health.

## Factory Farms

Besides the health issues associated with eating factory food, many people are **ethically** opposed to how the animals raised for fast and factory food are treated. The chickens used to make chicken nuggets and the cattle used to make hamburgers are often kept in terrible conditions. On factory farms, pigs are kept in crowded pens. Chickens who lay eggs are crowded into barns and kept in stacked cages. Even "free range" chickens live in small spaces. Cows and sheep raised for meat are fed hormones to make them gain weight in the form of muscle, fat, and other tissues more quickly.

Animals who are fed hormones and antibiotics suffer for most of their lives. This is where the phrase "you are what you eat" becomes important. When we eat meat or dairy products from animals raised in these conditions, we are ingesting everything they have eaten. Eating animals raised on factory farms can cause health problems and allergies in humans. Many people believe that food-producing animals should be raised and slaughtered without cruelty.

Overcrowding is an issue in large factory farms where animals have little room to move and diseases can spread quickly.

## Packaging Problems

Whole foods come in less packaging than factory foods—and less packaging means less pollution. Foods that are heavily

Many take-out and grocery store foods are packaged in single-use plastics that contribute to pollution.

processed also require a lot of energy to make and transport. According to the United Nations, food packaging makes up 5.4 percent of the greenhouse gas emissions that cause global climate change. Altogether, food systems are responsible for 34 percent of the world's greenhouse gas emissions. Choosing

**sustainably** packaged and produced foods is one way to help the planet.

Factory food usually comes in disposable wrappers. These wrappers take a long time to break down. The chemicals from the wrappers can leach into food and have effects on people's bodies. They can alter people's moods and overall health.

PFAs, or per- and polyfluoroalkyl substances, are other compounds used in food packaging to keep out heat, water, and oil. Many food wrappers, bags, containers, trays, plates, and boxes are made with PFAs. They transfer from these products to our bodies and the environment, where they build up over time. PFAs have polluted rainwater, soil, polar ice caps, oceans, plants, and animals, including humans. The health impacts of having PFAs in your body include higher risks of cancer and illnesses. High levels of PFAs have also been shown to worsen cases of COVID-19. Being mindful of how factory food packaging affects our health and the environment is another part of making healthy choices.

## Food for Thought

1. Food safety is regulated in restaurants and factories, but it's important everywhere. What food safety rules do you practice at home?
2. What are your beliefs about the ethics of raising, slaughtering, and eating animals? Are some methods more ethical than others?
3. Some big food companies are working to reduce their greenhouse gas emissions by 2030. What responsibility do food producers have to combat climate change?

Instead of sugary breakfast cereals, try starting the day with homemade oatmeal topped with fresh or frozen fruit and nuts.

# Chapter Four

## Healthy Choices

Making healthier food choices is a lifelong project that you can start at any time. You don't have to give up factory foods completely, but you can begin by swapping the least healthy factory foods you eat for more healthy whole foods. When you want a crunchy snack, grab an apple or some carrots instead of a bag of chips. Try replacing one serving of processed food each day with a handful of vegetables or a piece of fruit.

Look for whole foods and new flavors or textures that are interesting and exciting to you. You could ask a friend or family member to teach you a recipe from the culture they belong to. Recipes from a specific cultural tradition, such as Mediterranean or Indian, are more likely to use whole foods than processed foods as ingredients. You just might find your favorite new flavor combination!

### Healthy Breakfasts

There are more choices for breakfast than a box of sweetened cereal, processed into brightly colored shapes. A healthier option is to make homemade cereal using rolled oats and wheat germ. It only takes a few minutes to make, using a microwave or a kettle of boiling water. Fresh, dried, or frozen fruit is a great addition to plain yogurt. A breakfast wrap can be made with a whole-wheat tortilla wrapped around scrambled eggs, mushrooms, and diced peppers.

## Packing Lunch

Lunch is a good time to start replacing processed foods with whole foods. Lunch food doesn't have to be bought sealed in wrappers. It's not hard to make sandwiches with whole-grain bread. Cheese, boiled eggs, and raw vegetables are easy to slice up and enjoy. A casserole can be cut into individual portions and sealed in bowls with lids. That's also a good way to carry salads, with a separate container for dressing. A thermos can be used to

A homemade sandwich with fresh toppings can deliver protein, fiber, and vitamins to your meal. You can replace processed deli meat in your sandwich with hummus or egg salad.

carry homemade soup and keep it hot. There are bakeries that make muffins and cookies as good as homemade ones, with half the sugar, butter, and salt of most commercial baked goods.

## Snack Preparation

There are plenty of alternatives to a candy bar as a snack. Many so-called chocolate bars are actually made mostly of sugar or sweeteners manufactured from corn and are less than 12 percent chocolate. These bars don't melt on a warm day because **carnauba wax**, also used in shoe polish, is added. People who want to eat something sweet might choose an orange or piece of fruit instead. However, many stores don't sell fresh fruit, only processed sweets sealed in plastic wrappers.

It's easy to carry an apple or an orange for a snack. Other kinds of fruit such as peaches, bananas, or grapes may need to be

A handful of nuts is a nutrient-dense snack that will give you energy and satisfy your hunger between meals. Nuts have fiber, protein, and vitamins.

carried in a little container. Vegetables like beans and broccoli make tasty snacks too. There are tidy little bags of peeled carrots sold in grocery stores. It's fun to taste different fruits and vegetables as they become ripe each season.

There are salty alternatives to potato chips. One choice is natural popcorn: It's healthier when people buy a bag of kernels to pop. Microwave popcorn that is advertised as having "buttery" flavor is not made with real butter but a greasy additive with artificial ingredients. A bag of plain kernels is much less expensive too. Popcorn kernels can be microwaved in a paper bag or popped in a hot air popper. Popcorn tastes good plain, or you can drizzle a spoonful of melted butter or olive oil on top.

## Dinner Ideas

A fast dinner doesn't have to be take-out chicken or fast-food hamburgers, not when salads and roasts are easy to make. A good way to start is by replacing one processed dinner each week with a recipe you make from scratch. Making ordinary dinners out of whole foods gets easier with practice. There are cookbooks in libraries and many recipes online. Ask friends and relatives how to make special dishes—some people enjoy sharing recipes and cooking techniques.

A fun way to enjoy a number of different dishes is to hold a potluck dinner. When each person brings a different dish, no one person has to prepare the entire meal. Pizza parties are another fun idea for cooking with friends or family. Instead of having pizza delivered, start with homemade dough or a pack of whole-wheat tortillas. Add tomato sauce and some grated cheese. Let everyone top the pizzas with peppers, tomatoes, mushrooms, or their own favorites. Look for meat from animals raised on local farms.

Food is about more than just nutrition. It can also be about coming together as a family, neighborhood, or community.

## Food Choices

Parents feel responsible for choosing good food for their children's growing bodies. As young people grow up, they become responsible for making their own decisions about what to eat. It's hard to make good choices, though, when there are so many unhealthy options.

Around the country and the world, more governments are passing laws to help people make healthier choices. Some laws

## Eat Local

A good alternative to purchasing factory food that's been shipped across the country is to buy fresh food grown on local farms. Local food movements encourage people to enjoy seasonal foods that are locally grown by members of their own community—the closer they're grown to your home, the better!

Farmers markets bring fresh produce to customers in cities and towns and offer a fun way to get to know the people who make and grow your food. Visiting a farmers market might inspire you to try your hand at growing. Growing small pots of herbs on a windowsill is a good way to start. You can use these herbs to season the new recipes you try. You might be surprised at how flavorful they are!

Some restaurants focus on farm-to-table dining, bringing fresh ingredients from local farms right to your plate. Many grocery stores carry produce, meats, and dairy from the area. You might be able to find a CSA, which stands for Community Supported Agriculture. A CSA subscription gives you a regular supply of local produce or animal products and the challenge of using new and unfamiliar ingredients.

prohibit public schools from selling soft drinks or high-calorie, high-fat foods during school hours. Others ban certain ingredients or regulate sales and marketing in order to limit food ads that target children.

Although change is slow, factory food companies have responded to growing concerns about packaged factory food. Many large companies have committed to cutting calories in their foods and prioritizing whole food ingredients. Eating healthy doesn't have to mean giving up factory food entirely, but it can mean making smart choices about what you eat. The trend for healthy eating that's good for your body and good for the planet continues to grow. If customers ask for it, factories will work to

Even when fresh fruits and vegetables aren't available, frozen produce can provide healthy, whole food options.

make better food available, with healthier ingredients, clean processing, and less packaging.

## Food for Thought

1. Can you notice a difference between the taste of factory food and fresh, local food?
2. Some people think eating less fat, salt, and sugar means eating less tasty foods. Can you think of some natural fruits or vegetables that are flavorful and delicious on their own?
3. What local food options do you have where you live? Is there a farmers market or food co-op near your home?

# Glossary

**allergen:** A substance (usually protein) that causes an allergic response by the immune system, such as hives, swelling, stomachaches, hyperactivity, rashes, or problems breathing.

**calorie:** The unit of energy your body gets from food.

**carnauba wax:** A wax obtained from the leaves of the carnauba palm and commonly used in car wax, shoe polish, wood finishing, and low-priced candy bars.

**chronic:** Always present, as in a long-lasting disease or condition.

***Escherichia coli*:** A bacterium, *E. coli*, that lives in human and animal intestines and can cause mild diarrhea or no symptoms.

**ethical:** Related to a set of moral principles.

**fiber:** Bulky cells in plant matter that can absorb water or give a tough texture to food. It is indigestible but necessary for digestion of other food.

**fortified:** Made more nutritious with added ingredients.

**infection:** A disease caused by microorganisms such as bacteria, fungi, or viruses.

**pasteurize:** To use a heat treatment invented by Louis Pasteur to kill germs in milk or other foods without influencing the flavor or quality of the food.

**pathogen:** Something that produces a disease, such as a virus or bacterium.

**recall:** A public call by a manufacturer to return a contaminated food.

***Salmonella*:** A bacterium transferred from animals to humans through food that is not cooked thoroughly. It causes vomiting and severe diarrhea.

**sustainable:** Involving processes that don't destroy or completely use up the planet's natural resources.

**vitamin:** A nutrient, found in fruits, vegetables, grains, fungi, meats, and dairy foods, essential to the human body for health.

# Find Out More

## Books

Gunasekara, Mignonne. *Processed Foods: How People Are Poisoning Themselves, and What to Do About It*. King's Lynn, UK: BookLife Publishing, 2021.

Loh-Hagan, Virginia. *Food*. Ann Arbor, MI: Cherry Lake Publishing Group, 2021.

## Websites

**Food and Drug Administration**
*www.fda.gov/food*
The FDA regularly updates their website with information about food recalls, food safety, healthy diet recommendations, and nutrition facts.

***National Geographic Kids*: Indooor Herb Garden**
*kids.nationalgeographic.com/books/article/indoor-herb-garden*
This webpage from *National Geographic Kids* provides instructions for growing an indoor herb garden.

**World Health Organization**
*www.who.int/news-room/fact-sheets/detail/healthy-diet*
The World Health Organization provides guidance for people around the world on how to create a healthy, well-balanced diet.

## Organizations

**Action for Healthy Kids**
600 West Van Buren Street, Suite 720
Chicago, IL 60607
*www.actionforhealthykids.org*
Action for Healthy Kids works throughout the United States to educate people on the importance of healthy eating, exercise, and reducing childhood obesity.

**School Nutrition Association**
2900 South Quincy Street, Suite 700
Arlington, VA, 22206
*schoolnutrition.org/*
This nonprofit organization works to bring high-quality, nutritious meals to students in schools across the United States.

**Publisher's note to educators and parents:** Our editors have carefully reviewed these websites to ensure that they are suitable for students. Many websites change frequently, however, and we cannot guarantee that a site's future contents will continue to meet our high standards of quality and educational value. Be advised that students should be closely supervised whenever they access the internet.

# Index

# About the Author

**Rachael Morlock** is a freelance writer and copyeditor. She is the author of several nonfiction and picture books for children and enjoys researching new subjects through her work. In the past, she worked as the coordinator of a Community Supported Bakery. Rachael is always interested in supporting local farmers and food producers in Western New York, where she lives with her dog, Rilke.